The Tethers

in memory of my father,

Henry Ross Etter (1940-2009),

with love and gratitude

The Tethers
Carrie Etter

seren

Seren is the book imprint of
Poetry Wales Press Ltd.
57 Nolton Street, Bridgend, Wales, CF31 3AE
www.seren-books.com

The right of Carrie Etter to be identified as
the author of this work has been asserted in accordance
with the Copyright, Designs and Patents Act, 1988.

© Copyright Carrie Etter, 2009.

ISBN -978-1-85411-492-1

A CIP record for this title is available from the British Library.

The publisher acknowledges the financial assistance of the Welsh Books Council.

Cover Art: 'Discarding the Frame' by Mark Tansey. By kind permission of the
Gagosian Gallery

Printed in Bembo by Bell & Bain, Glasgow

Mixed Sources
Product group from well-managed
forests and other controlled sources
www.fsc.org Cert no. TT-COC-002769
© 1996 Forest Stewardship Council
FSC

Contents

"We lose everything, but make harvest of the consequence it was to us."

Jack Gilbert, 'Moreover'

Citizenship

If not the cheese festival, an open air concert
by the village's has-been rockers;
if not the May Day Dance, an impromptu wine tasting
on Murphy's return from Calais –

so I have become a global-warming adept,
an amateur meteorologist looking to,
nay beckoning extremes of heat and air,
frost and water, a day of reckoning for

everyone's favourite mayor, whose bad poetry
has become a feature of our weekly newsletter,
a column of O'Hara-derived frivolity beside
the irregular announcement of birth or death,

rarely in tandem in a population of two hundred and twelve.
I have refrained from Cassandraic warnings.
I have seen the man at his desk, giving up on Dostoevsky,
turning to plan the next amusement.

I am no god. I only want to believe in karma
in spite of the temperate spring,
in spite of his new wife
and the modesty of her pale blue shoes.

Ode to Raggedy Ann

Rag girl, limp limbs and stitched smile,
ludicrous in blue gingham, you are too
common for metaphor, too often not

just yourself, dowdy pinafore, button
black eyes, shoes as close as skin.
Who else has such red red hair,

such bossy features on a flat face?
No one, no one, I say, despite
the eyes' dull and dulling reflection,

the slackening in my legs, the slow burn
along each strand from scalp to shoulder,
darker than a blush, brighter than fire.

Biopsy

for Helen Pizzey

This is my body. This is my heart,
standing aside like a child at the zoo.

What thrives behind those rocks, those bars?
It has a name I can't pronounce.

Neither swift nor sluggish, it's
the child I myself have borne.

There is no one else to apologise to –
I'm sorry, I'm sorry – it could be a lullaby

if my breast were not both
body and heart.

Divorce

Forced to apologise
for the dirty sheets, he looks

proud in his shame.
I left that bed years ago

and have returned to collect
a forgotten book, a favourite blanket.

He knew the names of trees better
than makes of cars, but neither well.

He remembers which sister
I like least and asks

how she is doing.

Pleurisy

At the question
of lung capacity,

the radiator pops
and hisses, a fox

can only be metaphor.
You and that hunk

of metal wheeze.
Sixth floor, Manhattan,

six a.m. winter dark
looks like so much

air to be had.
The fox is stealth.

I almost miss it.

San Fernando Valley Love Song

for Jonathan Schwartz

Man of wax, my butterfly days rode in your pocket:
flutter and fluster, a girl on a daisy, an open electrical socket.
You strummed the valley's grid, chord to chord,
while I relished all the mangoes I could afford.

Man of wax, my butterfly days never knew a gold locket:
corn husk, thrift shop, paperback, pop-can rocket.
You tie-dyed-cotton, you backpack-playwright,
you marvelled at the string for my red brick kite.

Man of wax, my butterfly days are down to this docket:
lace mittens, tumbleweed, unsweetened chocolate.
We dervished among the palms, the stars below,
city lights, one night, last night, so long ago.

Horace's Wet Clothes

after Ode I.5

Shipwrecked sailors hung their shirts, still dripping,
on the temple wall. Poseidon's temple,

it faces the sea, faces Poseidon, the presumably
not arbitrary god who saved them.

Now Horace, teeth rattling in the wake
of a fickle girl's black-cold wind,

wanders the cape and finds the temple of tunics.
In a breath, he is bare-chested,

spirited by metaphor: the acrid wave, the wreck,
and one relenting god.

Talking with Beccaria

Sit with me, Beccaria. On the basis
of your reputation as an illustrious bore,
I've saved you a chair in this dim corner
complete with a bowl of mixed nuts
so we need not rise for ponderous hours.

I have watched the mistress of scintillation
with her magenta shoes and thin fingers
preside even in selected minutes of remission
with a laugh that falls like a wood-splitting axe,
with the gaze of the panopticon's unseen guard.

All the while my chuckle tumbled into her stream,
my chatter leapt into her sonorous silences
until the night overwhelmed our attenuating umbrellas
to send us singly home. My pallor was not loss but guilt
for the self I regretted spurning even as I knew

I would spurn it again. I would spurn it again.

Axes for Crutches

Once, the view from this room cost twenty guineas.
Once, the view discerned the hangman
selling his rope by the inch.

On the Underground, a drugged girl swayed,
palms pressed to hold open the doors
between rush-hour carriages.

The remarking crowd refuses an exit.
The train will never stop.

Something is using axes for crutches,
breaking the earth's crust as it goes.

Seaborne

Buoys and lifeboats, inflatable vests and detachable cushions
order the map of fear with routes of survival.

Yet it is enough to find Polonius's end plausible,
the accidents that follow negligible peccadilloes,

it is enough to see Gertrude's change of feeling
as ordinary and therefore the more monstrous,

to know I am the one who drowns in a temperate sea
blind to the outstretched rope in the dread of its absence.

Cult of the Eye

Then I glanced over the treetops, the miles of pasture
the window shows me again and again,
and soon I began to believe the window;
I became a votary in the cult of the eye and the cult
of transparency, because after we spoke
I used a form of to be as an equal sign: you were transparent.
I gleefully forbore the scepticism of *seemed*.

Admittedly, I nearly said you *appeared* transparent,
but I put my ear to the window's mantra
and asseverated your sincerity without reserve.
If this is a love poem, that's because I'm ready to love everybody.
I'll gaze on the miles of pasture as the sun descends
and never think I must kneel in the dampening grass;
and you'll refrain, just for now, from remarking my naiveté.

David Smith, *Wagon II*, 1964

A figure sleeps standing because the wagon it rides
never rolls on its diverse wheels, is carried

from studio to museum and back by no
motive of its own, or at least none it knows.

The steel's tremendous weight is at odds
with its curves, their expectation of velocity.

Sometimes the wagon supposes it emerged as is,
fully formed, one of the angels,

till it remembers the message etched on its largest wheel,
a greeting from maker to daughter – *Hi, Candida!* –

that lessens the vehicle's gravitas
and gravity, as if with a light push....

The Assenting Castaway

After you tossed my mooring down the well,
I floated through days like a Mylar balloon:
I began aloft and rising, but in seventy-two hours
I sagged like an old woman's breast.

Nor did mirrors yearn in your absence.
I would not have it so.
I prize the Cyclops with his discerning eye
foremost on the barker's catalogue of freaks.

If I put my ear to the stone circumference, I hear
my tether clanking all the way down – and up again.
One month's oxen-drag through the rocky field
becomes the next month's meadow-stroll,

the flint in my pockets anchorage or trail markers
to lead you home. Tell me which. Tell me both.

Collecting the Ridges

The skyline geometry and the April fog are again at odds. This prompts me, as usual, to go and stand on Hungerford Bridge to collect ridges of riverwater. Once the commuter exodus has passed, the god of the Thames – for it is too dark to lack a god – goes to his timpani and starts a tremor of sound. I stare harder to hear it. An hour into my work, a group of tourists asks me to take their picture a second time: in the first, they saw nothing they could name.

Four Hours from the Coast

The motels whose neon vacancy signs
blink drowsily at the oncoming cars,

whose olive sinks sputter rusty water,
whose suspicious vending machines carry

a childhood candy believed obsolete,
dim a day's accomplishment: We made it

this far? It is not that we cannot hear
the surf at this distance, but we begin

to doubt it can thrive within tomorrow's
enervated reach, just a day away

from the bedspread's unhealthily brown blooms.
A breeze at the open window does not

flutter the curtain and smells nothing of
the sea. We dine in the only café,

where we sip weak coffee from mismatched mugs,
name-drop our destination to assure

any listeners we're going somewhere.

The Colony of Us

Someone treads the thin carpet of the evacuated flat above –
yesterday the shopping trolley at its door refilled in motley surges
as though its driver purchased in anticipation of natural disaster,
hurricane or holiday.

On with the morning news, up with the volume. The pipes?
The pipes, or the wind. Else we have celebrated our solitude in vain.
Else the emptied bottle left standing wears its ornate label
like a vanquished flag.

Too soon we have drained the creak and stomp of human feeling.
Despite the trolley's marathon of laps, the parting sneer
we perceived through our own drawn, dark curtain,
we are less and less alone,

however the world would seem to relinquish us.

The Review

So at Starbuck's you stood in line
behind The Review's assistant managing editor?
A skinny cappuccino? Were you close enough
to detect her brand of shampoo?
There is no need to name The Review:
it is the one that, when mentioned, inclines all bystanders
toward its vocalization until they ascertain
the nature of the allusion and proceed accordingly.
If you are an author whose work appears in the current issue,
at least two well-scented women will brush your arm 'inadvertently'
and one man will strive to prolong your stay in his presence
with a look of surpassing interest.
Publication in a past issue creates a circle
of brightened eyes, however nonchalant some try to act,
and a member of the opposite sex will ask
what you're having and bring you another
whatever the volume in your present glass.
If The Review has never accepted your work
and you live in the same city as its offices,
once a month you will find yourself unaccountably
walking past the building's reflective panels and steel yourself
to look only ahead until you reach the end of the street,
but alas! you glance in The Review's direction to see
an image of yourself that seems disparagingly untrue.
Some neglected authors cannot stop thinking of The Review:
they can recount the highlights of senior editors' résumés,
and a simple 'Sorry' handwritten on the rejection slip
gives them days of delight, even though they suspect
a mere intern has so condescended. A mere intern!
No one at The Review is mere. The janitor may know
whose manuscript lingers on whose desk.
The Review's aura has an impressive breadth.
Even I feel giddy from speaking so long of it.

The Daughters of Prospero

When gales make a house a boat to toss on water,
and Gonzalo scrutinizes me, says I'm ripe

for hanging, and loquaciously heads below deck,
I know this isn't the oceanic feeling

Freud wrote of, this lingering image of a child
placing paper boat after boat onto a brook,

though each one drowns in a short drop ten feet downstream.
Placing white boat after boat onto a brook,

because she has learned beginner's origami,
because her fingers have amassed a score of cuts,

because some of the boats never looked seaworthy,
because a surprising number can glide like swans,

the girl sets her boats on a fatal course, and though
her head is bent, I can just see her eyes' fierce gleam.

The Tethers

for Matt Bryden

Hyacinth by orangutan by protozoa, you build our new earth.
Your fingers lift each species from the old solarium with care,
though you scatter them over the nascent world a little recklessly.
This Noah gathers not merely specimens but the lot, the better
to maintain the chains of predator and prey, parasite and host.
Even so, you should give resettlement more thought: the gazelle
in the British Library plaza may find the vegetation limited.

Think of the childlike couple on Underground posters
telling us to relinquish our seats to the aged and avoid
the shows of force in boisterous earphones and fried food.
Despite the absence of genitalia, one child's long, wispy hair
and distinct eyelashes, the other's short, thick mop gender them.
We don't know who we are without sex, and you'll compound
or mitigate the gazelle's displacement by adding a mate.

You're thinking human population: two, but others will emerge
to lead the gazelles to water, to unlock the library's doors,
to pull pints of Timothy Taylor and take down a packet of peanuts.
If you dread that a few weeks may undermine your grand design,
that you'll recognize only what was in the abundance that is,
remember that we live by lacing between past and present
stronger, straighter tethers than can possibly hold.

As your first draft nears completion, as my hand falls on your thigh,
the children's cherub plumpness and apparent distaste for dress
suggest a return from the various world to *homo desiderans*,
to our own naked bodies, self as both tenor and vehicle,
never wholly unmade but in constant flux with the expiring
and transpiring of cells in the relentless reformation of skin,
not to mention the teeming death and life of the interior.

Over the moors, a break between clouds amid their easy stroll
instills a wide band of light that skims the hills, wakens their green
briefly before it slumbers again in shadow. The world is ever
on the move. If I stayed this new earth you did and did not make –
but I would not, not even to allow your sigh's passage, your heart's pause.
The heart cannot pause. If we're not sexless children, neither are we
so innocent as we make and break, make and break each other.

Millais' Ophelia

Twilight into dusk, Ophelia's bridal gown
gains in severity what it loses in splendour.
If the sun descends outside the Tate,

inside, the diminished daylight
influences the act of interpretation.
There is a London-winter hermeneutic at work

well into April, and a twenty-some couple,
so serious as they near the exchange of keys,
talk in turn, halting yet vigorous

as they manage to skirt the word
tragedy, to say nothing of love.

Siren

Your sonorous voice rode the crests of foam
spraying along the boat's length, cool water misting
the rowers' sunburned shoulders. As my mouth opened
into a sigh, half-chagrin, half-relief at my security,
my torso bound to the mast to fortify virtue, one drop
smacked my brow and raced to wet my parted, parched lips.

I arched my back, the coarse bonds across my chest
easily yielded, and your naked body rose on a closing reef.
Before the boat struck rock, already I heard its wood planks
cracking, splitting, splintering and realised from your endless refrain
that the crash of bodies was not a song you wrote for me,
but the only words you knew. And still I sailed for you.

Almandine

Although she married twelve years after Keats died, Fanny
Brawne wore the engagement ring he gave her until her death.

Since Louis hasn't asked, I have
    not told. I am discreet –
I clean it only when alone,
    rubbing the boxy beet

red stone into a dark mirror.
    Some law prohibits this:
on the left hand, a wedding band;
    the right's ring a promise

unfulfilled. Married, I am still
    engaged. I did not choose.
Or that is not a ring there, but
    the past's persisting bruise.

Fin de Siècle

It's not that the water isn't potable, but only a few stars come down to earth now, and by ones and threes opera goers linger in the dark house. They settle back into their seats around midnight, staring forward as though an encore will soon begin. Afternoons, children sit on the ground next to the birch, positioning themselves so that if they were but eight feet higher, they'd perch on the five stout boughs hacked to stumps last week. They try to perfect a way of slackening their legs, now drooping, now bending, but their legs will not dangle and swing. The grandfather hastens the children home yet remains after they are gone, gazing at the invisible boughs and reaching up as though he would brush the bark with his fingertips, if he were just tall enough.

Indian Summer

Here friends revel in dandelion wine and watery sunsets,
white wicker and a sense of strewn threads interweaving
into a single opulent tapestry, while the dregs of wine
recall what we discreetly, half-wittingly neglect.

In the day-end danger, its vague desperation, we play at
defining infidelity, trying to name what faithfulness originates
in our private splendours. We waver among complacency,
trepidation, excitement. My palms sweat while my calves stretch.

Another's consciousness has never seemed so remote or so close.
The twilight gradually dims as its source recedes,
and the windows begin to misrepresent faces, unwrinkled if pale,
beautiful if spectral, and therefore unmistakably ours.

Arcadia, or Something Like It

after Bob Dylan's 'Who Killed Davey Moore?' and Virgil's first eclogue

Before everyone excused themselves of the boxer's death,
Arcadia, or something like it, prospered. Two shepherds met
under a beech's ample canopy.

One, prostrate on the summer grass, spoke in the drawl of leisure.
The other stood with his back against the sun; he spoke
of the soldiers gifted with his land

and lamented his imminent emigration.
The pipe-player replied with apples, chestnuts,

curdled milk, the bounty that would satisfy
those who were sated.

Americana, Station by Station

At our lowest price today only
vote Appelman for the school board
the Lakers beating San Antonio by 39 points
your sins will be forgiven

on mattresses all your favorite brands
because as a teacher he knows
in the fourth quarter a few minutes to go
so long as you accept Christ as your lord

name-brand comfort at a great value
what students need and parents want
yet another rebound – let's see that again
you are saved, I tell you, you are saved

Arizona, 2002

On the tongue, an impalpable sweetness,
as though the cactus's iridescent blue flower
has poured a thimble of its nectar into
the dry air, has given up just enough
of its cache to compel us to loiter at this
roadside stand, to pick up and turn the same
terracotta jug, the same turquoise bracelet.

We must look tempted. The sign's slashes
of red paint promise real Indian crafts,
with real underscored twice to assert
authenticity. My hands are so pale.
Behind the makeshift counter, the dark teen
daughter of the standkeepers (so she seems)
gazes in my direction, looks beyond me.

Days in Mladá Boleslav

July 2007

Here, any talisman is a broken compass,
its needle indeterminate between East and West –

the greased-salt smell of McDonald's fries,
the soft-while-firm comfort of dumplings,
and the high-pitched shrieks of a common bird.

★

In the square mile before the factory gates,
panelak after panelak in concrete monotony.

A third up the largest windows, a steel rod
is to keep occupants from falling forward, falling out.

★

In many blocks, each flat has a balcony, its posts
often wrapped with corrugated aluminium.

And each has use: a two-by-five-foot garden;
a laundry, its clothes dry in hours;

or a smokers' room, the banister bearing
all a body's weight from the elbows.

★

Friday evening, no one leans on a balcony –
they're all at this or another hospoda,
on a second half-litre of Gambrinus or Pilsner.

Seven-thirty – still light for a couple hours
and still essentially sober, though perhaps
talk's pace has quickened; perhaps tonight,

every remark has its response.

★

The hill at Kosmonosy gives, in the distance,
a view of 'Panelak City,' tight cluster

of a hundred concrete towers, or, looking down,
a meadow of weed and wildflower.

★

Across from the factory, the motley stores
of cheap wares: shampoo, bric-a-brac, bras,

plastic toys, t-shirts with slogans in English.
In this shop, five young Chinese, descendants

of another era, bustle from day-lit room to room.
On the pavement, two grandmothers mutter –

they knew shops like these decades ago
and have something to say about 'presidential vision.'

★

Let's go to the Škoda museum –
not the one behind glass, the one

stretched in a row before each street of panelaks,
the models becoming older the farther one goes

from the factory.

★

Ten o' clock, the sky just darkening,
the heat still on, the workers, unspeaking,

surge toward the factory gates;
Czech, Slovak, Turkish, singly and grouped –

ten minutes and the stream doesn't dwindle.

Fear of Lightning

Welcome to your monastery, now a secular retreat,
font of post-America.
Aren't these ordinary mishaps, not
sacrilege per se –

step on a pavement's inevitable cracks;
neglect to bed
your pillow on a geranium leaf; stroll, Escher-style,
under ladders –

a reflexive cause and effect ensue, a doctor's hammer
striking your knee;
is taken for naturalism, as much as my long hair's
whitened by years.

In the Czech Republic, report goes, sixty-nine percent
deny or doubt godhood,
but when I open my red-yet-leopard-print umbrella
indoors, no one's

questioning the colour. What thought never quite emerges
as you bend and bend again,
bowing to no one, you say, no one, as if with repetition
you could believe.

Soporific Red

The high street reddens with holiday,
and in your want of a rudder, the abundant dye
seeps upward, colours your trouser cuffs.

Already you wonder whether you'll have to pay
for the unordered dish, the neighbourhood flavour.
Already you're keen to roll it on your tongue.

On the fifth day of rain, home truths
seem irrelevant. It's a soporific red
divining the high street, blinding your hands.

It's a siren, ineluctable, inaudible, at your ear.

Lecture

One student's mysticism
depended on the affection of giraffes,
while another's derived
from the recurring grip of déjà vu.
The professor yawned
with a camel's slow insolence.

With increasing vigour the professor recounted
Freud's attack on "oceanic feeling"
while some reluctantly, some avidly
took notes. I had no fondness for giraffes
nor psychoanalysis, so I listened
with dismissive boredom

and watched the girl who spoke
of souls in all creatures
breaking pencils in her lap one by one
through a once inexhaustible supply.

The Lengthening Winter

Snow flurries induce
      lethargy, the house more sluggishly still
            for the bustle around and over it

Green is
      elsewhere; here each branch of the birch
            flails, reawakened to its loss

Someone will return,
      but for now acres of prairie succumb to the weight
            of air emptied of the living,

where I, alone in a house
      alone on frozen fields, wander by windows
            to manifest the ghost

of the human

Hardscrabble

This is the cobbled street, these the blistered soles.
Snow makes one feel one's bones beneath
the here overtender, here callused flesh.
By the seventh day, even the youngest
bones feel brittle.

Ranged around the meeting table, we are so many
near-misses of disaster, columnar testaments
to resilience and weather. Into the second hour,
I yearn to read anything but most of all
a few exquisite lines.

Come away, come away! In Celsius,
just two more degrees feels like a reprieve;
but already I am peeling off a scarf,
exposing more skin to accommodate my sense
of the impossible.

Bared hands open in the cracking wind.

Early Days

With such unfamiliar bounty, there's no saying
the date of harvest, or even what harvest would mean

when, no larger than thimbles, little older than the morning,
these fruits suffuse the tongue with a sweetness that never cloys.

Ask the month of harvest, ask the month of their decline –
I know what you ask. Persephone learned that ripening hues

mean more than death, or so I tell her story. Today I'll describe
the taste with Jamesian flourish. Bring your own words.

The Violet Hour

Fiesta Grande RV Resort, Casa Grande, Arizona

Whether the violet hour descends
or ascends, the aged cannot say. They are sure
that the horizon's fading flamboyance
is a colour at once at the world's edge
and suffusing the general air at such a dilution
that they sip it almost imperceptibly.

A lawn-chair lecture slowly coalesces
to enforce my lesser age. I nod at the horizon
to appease, to annoy, to acknowledge.
At the periphery, a raccoon noses
the toppled pail, the day's remains.
Already I am not seeing him.

Lowers, says one. *Or trickles.*
Someone suggests going for *Roget's*,
but the shift of bodies, rasp of the chairs' joints
only settle us in our makeshift amphitheatre,
only resolve us not to choose between
the rise and fall of what we cannot moor.

Late Winter, Early Year

The blinds closed against sunset, no sunset today;
      come again another, an indolent day.
We are collating the depositions, the testimonials, a Babel
      of paling sentiment – is that the smell of salt water

or regret? The blinds closed to divert the sublime,
      possible, irremediable nonchalance.
We are taking numbers, taking turns, taking the trouble,
      differentiating between sleep and slumber,

stagger and sidle. The blinds closed to enclose this
      small room, one emptied, filling pocket.
I think I smell music, violin or tambourine. I think
      the horizon must be nearly gold, as close as it gets.

The Wake

Santa Monica Mountains, 1993

The hills rise blackly,
charred tree by tree.

Where no squirrel forages
or bird nests, where

no leaf absorbs
the noon light,

the silence refuses
peace to the traveller,

who feels at once
guilty to pass and

guilty to pause.

The Trapeze Artist's Dear John Letter

I recede like a vanishing point on my ribboned trapeze
and trust hamstring and calf's steady marriage
when I hang from my knees.

Physics can name the force that pushes the bar away again.
I'd call it *Fortune's wheel* or *Tantalus's fruit,*
but then I'm the company tragedienne –

all good trapeze artists are. I no sooner arrive than leave.
I love you, I'm quitting you. I live my life between
the two meanings of cleave.

The Separation

for Susan Mackervoy

The diaphragm flattens and holds.
My sister, twenty-seven, offers a medal of St Christopher.
My friend loses another earring between her floorboards.

The tongue tucks behind the teeth.
My niece, four, asks when I'll come down from the sky.
My friend and I imagine future anthropologists, interpreting the hoard.

The feet perceive the extra miles.
My mother, fifty-eight, voices true and untrue platitudes,
        one and the same.
My ring knows the way to the foundation.

The hair swings because it can.
My nephew, six, says the world will go on long after he's dead.
Someone will find the diamond and see in its clarity the colour of loss.

Postmarked (Ars Poetica)

Royal Mail's Mount Pleasant Sorting Office in London
is one of the largest such offices in the world.

Shouting silently in the operating theatre,
I become multiple, as all pandemonium's angels
arose from one idea.

Later at Mount Pleasant, neither mountain nor,
I hover over slicing letters, parcels tumbling
between destinations.

I discern my own estranged members,
more than parings if less than limbs.
A dungeon's devices

are indistinguishable from early surgical tools.
I am coming home, I am leaving for good with no
expectation of rest.

At last the day is sorted. Whether growths
or creations, my chattels jostle in their sacks
and renounce me.

The Bonds

What wharf has neither metal anchor nor heavy coils of rope?
Farther down the Thames is a bridge once favoured
by prostitutes for its low guardrail, the ease of descent,
though other, unmentioned girls came to prop a heel
on its cold steel and so divulge a shapely calf.

Which is to say that a search of the dock would find the usual
instruments of restraint, but of such strange material
that though their forms would foster recognition, you'd yearn
to touch them, to weigh in a palm the anchor that could not
pin a bird, the rope as light as a mouthful of fruit.

Hard science might explain the boat's fidelity by reckoning the waves'
relative stillness, the craft's weight, the distance of the moon.
And as for 'soft' science, the -ologies of more elusive chemistries,
leave them to speak amongst themselves with a shrug
of your pale shoulders, with the memory of one deepening kiss.

The Honeymoon of Our Attraction

The honeymoon of our attraction subsided abruptly,
as though after a summer in a beach cottage I resumed
the urban and a drinking spout's arc became the only water
I put my mouth to.

If then I'd painted the seaside town from memory, I'd have chosen
watercolours for the streaks of illumination become impalpable.
Incarnate rode the subway stink, the traffic din, the elusive
beauty of passing faces.

Yet months later the dune grasses, smelling of transience,
smelling of risk, scratch my palms with their long blades.
Where did they come from? Of the wave's surge I know only
I stand soddened.

The Sty

My left eye shucks old shadow from its lid like my mother
shucks corn – no pity for the cob, no love for the husk,
and when that eye drools a lash as though it's the last paper boat
childhood will sail down the stream,

you'd expect me to quake, and truly the right instrument
would have registered significant fault line activity
when I saw the curtains inch toward centre stage to eclipse
the opera's vermilion and verdant velvets, the soprano's mole

that becomes a black hole, the Bermuda Triangle
of identity as I know it, so certainly my doctor's mild tone
heralds a potential treachery and spurs me
on the first crack of the door to hurtle away

with my handful of limes, I mean my prescription
on lime-coloured paper that induces a desire to see limes *now*,
to gawk at a grocer's pile of variegated green to the utmost
of my hindered ability because I have failed to memorize

my husband's face any better than I recall the opening
of Chaucer's prologue, vigorously reciting four lines
and brokenly another four until I gasp at *foweles*,
but as I close on the chemist's before I locate a fruit vendor,

my entrance knocks the overhead bell, the bell clinks
rather prosaically, and that sound provides enough sustenance
to propel me to the counter and the chemist who would regard
blood trickling the length of my torso with nonchalance

and who answers my alarm with disdain – well, I wish it were disdain
so I could despise him, but he responds with a voice as bland
as cafeteria tuna casserole that he cannot specify how many days
I must wait, and as I fear to ask of the point-one percent I suspect

wait with no relief, I clutch my odds and look askance at the bright-eyed
until I slam the door of my empty flat, empty of that husband
whose face even now I muster as the auspicious drop swims
over cornea and sclera with an ease that's exhilaration, I mean

exhalation – which is to say exaltation, of the eye and the larks it can see.

Vermilion

Tell me about the lie, how it seems to begin in necessity but later looks like self-indulgence. The garden was choking on weeds, and the lie offered itself as a strong pair of hands. The fluorescent tubes gave a ghoulish cast to my face, and the lie appeared to light my skin from within, a shimmer of health. Show the plant roots loosened by the weeds' plunder, the new lines about my eyes. The old greed is returning, its velvet cape a beguiling sweep of colour.

Magnum Opus

Bracken, brambles, and bindweed obscure my castle
that would otherwise gleam in the midday sun.
I hauled the rock hither. I carved it into blocks.
I studied the history of architecture before I set a stone.

Perhaps gleam exaggerates the image.
Perhaps the walls' pallor appears a sheer white
under the encroaching summer, and the buttresses
bear few but portentous fissures.

The castle also lacks a good bed, which is to say
that once I hack through this derisive vegetation,
I will mount the highest turret and wave my arm in grand sweeps.
I may hire some extras or bribe my friends to stand below.

I may drag the miles of bindweed down the corridors,
up the stairwells, and burn, burn, burn my fortress through.
Then may the pundits come and mourn.
Then may I lie on a kind mattress and dream of bungalows.

Over the Thames

If sadness began the bridge, a buttress
for the arc over the river, some would trust
the traversing more.

I would. How many let the newspaper graze
their foreheads to wear the ink communally,
to make an anthem

of a private dirge? I cannot name the tethers
that hold the curve taut, the path's
line straight from

bank to bank: there is no universal
for what keeps us aloft, but O
I cherish it.

Crowd of One

For minutes, sometimes hours, a single tap
deftly splits the egg, yolk and white slide out,
the shell closes on air and arcs
in its flight to the bin. Synapses fire palpably.
Regret is elsewhere.
Light suffuses the room, without any discrete source.

The World at Dusk

Along the lanes, in the emerging day,
a body in the world is a body
on an errand. The aching calf
knows the passage of time.

Injury once left me long
on the window's warmer side, gazing
at the snow blown through
the poplars' leafless branches.

All day, each day, the world was at dusk,
the change of light incidental.
When at last I walked to the postbox, afternoon
was everywhere. I had decades to live.

Acknowledgements

Thanks to the editors of these publications, where the poems herein first appeared: *Columbia: A Journal of Literature and Art, Leviathan Quarterly, The Liberal, Meridian, Metre, The New Republic, New Welsh Review, New Writing 14* (Granta, 2006), *PN Review, Poetry London, Poetry Review, Poetry Wales, The Republic of Letters, The Rialto, Stand, Thumbscrew, The Times Literary Supplement, The Warwick Review.*

Thanks are also due to the editors of the following publications, where some of these poems were reprinted: *All That Mighty Heart: London Poems* (University of Virginia Press, 2008), *Blue Arc West: An Anthology of California Poets* (Tebot Bach, 2006), *The Forward Book of Poetry 2005* (Forward/Faber, 2004), *Limelight, Eyewear, Faultline, Orange Coast Review, Women's Work: Modern Women Poets Writing in English* (Seren, 2009).

I also wish to note my gratitude to the University of California, Irvine for a Leona B. Gerard Fellowship in Creative Writing and a Humanities Pre-doctoral Fellowship. Both proved important in seeing this work to fruition.

Thanks to the following friends whose unrelenting faith sustained me through the work on the manuscript: Moniza Alvi, Simon Avery, Lynn Corr, Francesca Francoli, Tony Frazer, Kathryn Gray, Karen Hoy, Susan Mackervoy, Lytton Smith, Greta Stoddart, and Alan Summers. Matt Bryden and Claire Crowther have my gratitude for their passionate support and instructive responses to the manuscript, and I am indebted to Tim Liardet for his generous and insightful assistance with the final revisions.

Lastly, I have been fortunate in having the ardent support of family, friends, and students, whom I thank heartily for seeing me here.

About the Author

After spending her first nineteen years in Normal, Illinois, Carrie Etter travelled to Los Angeles on a one-way train ticket and lived in southern California for the next thirteen years. There she completed a BA in English at the University of California, Los Angeles and an MFA in creative writing at the University of California, Irvine. In 2001 she moved to England, and in 2003 UC Irvine awarded her a PhD in English for her work in Victorian literature and culture. She lives in Bradford on Avon and teaches as a lecturer in creative writing at Bath Spa University.